ALMOST THE EQUINOX:
SELECTED POEMS

ALMOST THE EQUINOX
Selected Poems

Sarah Maguire

Chatto & Windus
LONDON

1 3 5 7 9 10 8 6 4 2

Chatto & Windus, an imprint of Vintage,
20 Vauxhall Bridge Road,
London SW1V 2SA

Chatto & Windus is part of the Penguin Random House group of companies
whose addresses can be found at global.penguinrandomhouse.com

Penguin
Random House
UK

First published by Chatto & Windus in 2015

www.vintage-books.co.uk

A CIP catalogue record for this book is available from the British Library

ISBN 9780701188559

Typeset by Palimpsest Book Production Limited, Falkirk, Stirlingshire
Printed and bound by Clays Ltd, St Ives plc

Penguin Random House is committed to a sustainable future for our business, our
readers and our planet. This book is made from Forest Stewardship
Council® certified pa

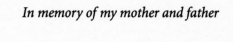

In memory of my mother and father

Contents

First publication is listed after each poem's title as follows:
SM: *Spilt Milk* (1991); *IM*: *The Invisible Mender* (1997); *FM*: *The Florist's at Midnight* (2001); *PK*: *The Pomegranates of Kandahar* (2007)

ALMOST THE EQUINOX:
SELECTED POEMS

Cloves and Oranges

My souvenir of Taliouine
was oranges: three oranges
to bring this place to mind.
They glowed like pumpkin-lanterns
in the garden in the dark

on the last tree by the house;
their luminous skin
aromatic and oily and waxed.
Not quite oranges,
some cross-breed grafted on –

a scar on the trunk
where the damaged cambium
had swollen with healing.
The glossy, oval leaves.
The plump fruits secret in the leaves.

I woke that night
in my white-painted tower
with its three small windows
and knew I'd not come back:
the huge stars hammered

in the sky,
the Atlas mountains folded in sleep,
the river bed
rustling with bamboo.
I will never come back.

In London I ate one of the oranges,
split one with a friend,
left the other in the bowl.
Oh, they were sharp!
like hybrid grapefruit,

too tart for eating.
But the third
I studded full of cloves.
Each tiny crucifixion
a fizz of oil through the skin,

as, pore by pore,
I pressed the clove-nails in,
till the whole globe
bristled with small woody buds.
I looped a ribbon round it

and hung the final orange
from a nail.
Memory is smell.
Next winter,
night by night,

I'll loosen one clove,
then the next.
I'll burn them,
one by one,
till the fruit is bald and gone.

The Pomegranates of Kandahar

The bald heft of ordnance
A landmine
shrapnel cool in its shell

Red balls
pinioned in pyramids
rough deal tables stacked to the sky

A mirrored shawl
splits
and dozens tumble down –

careering through the marketplace
joyful fruit
caught by the shouts of barefoot children

Assembled, they are jewels –
jewels
of garnet, jewels of ruby

A promise deep as the deep red of poppies
of rouged lips (concealed)
Proud hearts

built of rubble
Come, let us light candles in the dust
and prise them apart –

thrust your knife through the globe
then twist
till the soft flesh cleaves open

to these small shards of sweetness
Tease each jellied cell
from its white fur of membrane

till a city explodes in your mouth
Harvest of goodness,
harvest of blood

Psoriasis

After all this time on my knees
I am starting to bleed –

the cushion, the dark sheets
are foxed with my dead skin

worn from love
from the way you move me,

the cream dust like meal,
spoor in the tracks.

Again you kneel back
to look at me like this

opened before you, patient
your hand encircling my ankle.

It has rained all afternoon,
the light stipple of water on glass

seeps into my breathing,
your musk on my lips.

I lay my cheek on the pillow
to take you in

I could be a child again
suckling my own thumb.

Psoriasis

If a red rose lies at the heart of me,
it cannot bloom.

Speechless, unknown –
but for this roseate

plague on my knuckles
and knees,

shedding its bastard pollen
in my sheets;

colourless,
the wrong pain.

Psoriasis

At five-and-a-half the skin on my knees
turned to paper and flaked off.
I would peel away the scales
and lay them on the window-sill –
each a milky carapace fretted with pores.
It was still light. I could hear
the older children hiding
and finding each other again.
I put all my toys in the bed
and slept on the floor.

No-one went out now.
My father's hip-bone was crumbling away.
They had taken him to the hospital
and opened it up like an egg;
at its core was an abscess
the doctor plucked out.
One afternoon I watched him asleep,
his hands gathering the eiderdown.

My mother was frightened.
I get on a bus and I just can't breathe.
When I broke the tea-cup she locked
herself in the bathroom for hours.
I squeezed under my bed
and traced its paisley mattress
with my finger – the swirls and flowers
fell into themselves, repeating
and repeating into the dark.
I wondered where the pattern began.

The Invisible Mender (My First Mother)

I'm sewing on new buttons
to this washed silk shirt.
Mother-of-pearl,
I chose them carefully.
In the haberdasher's on Chepstow Place
I turned a boxful over
one by one,
searching for the backs with flaws:
those blemished green or pink or aubergine,
small birth marks on the creamy shell.

These afternoons are short,
the sunlight buried after three or four,
sap in the cold earth.
The trees are bare.
I'm six days late.
My right breast aches so
when I bend to catch a fallen button
that strays across the floor.
Either way,
there'll be blood on my hands.

Thirty-seven years ago you sat in poor light
and sewed your time away,
then left.
But I'm no good at this:
a peony of blood gathers on my thumb, falls
then widens on the shirt like a tiny, opening mouth.

I think of you like this –
as darkness comes,
as the window that I can't see through
is veiled with mist
which turns to condensation
slipping down tall panes of glass,
a mirror to the rain outside –
and I know that I'll not know
if you still are mending in the failing light,
or if your hands (as small as mine)
lie still now, clasped together, underground.

The Hearing Cure

I dunk my head
under water
and come up
deaf. My left ear

solid, as though
half the world
is moored in perspex.
My life

bifurcates. I turn
around
and a jellied stillness
drags behind me,

an abeyance of rustling,
mortality hushed.
The rope of blood
twists

in my ear, plaiting
and unplaiting,
the world gone
bone.

Each night
the slow wax silts
into place
coagulating sibilance,

muffling susurration,
the soft moraine
lagging the tympanum,
secluding

stirrup, hammer, anvil
in a distant room.
The plug is full.
When I was three

sound turned to stone,
then festered;
my skull became
a labyrinth of pain,

my taut throat
stuffed
with liquid needles.
That winter afternoon

you pushed my cot
into the warm front room
and soothed me on your lap.
There was the red wool

of your jumper
unravelling
at one wrist,
your kind heart

marking time. By tea
it was dark outside;
the football results
came on the radio;

Scottish League Division Two –
Stirling Albion,
Cowdenbeath,
Montrose, Arbroath,

Dunfermline,
Heart of Midlothian,
Queen of the South –
a litany

that lulled me
into sleep.
I left you
twenty years ago.

Since then
we've hardly talked –
until I found you
shrunken, frightened,

speechless
on a geriatric ward,
your legs gone dead
from grief:

you couldn't stand it
when your brother died.
And now you cling to me
for dear life,

your wasted,
beautiful hands
slim messengers of fear.
Weeks on,

you start to tell me things
I've never heard before,
all that silence
frozen in your limbs.

But when we got you home
we found
they hadn't bathed you
for a month

because you'd not complain,
not ask, not bother anyone.
It made me sick.
And now I'm ill, bewildered,

lonely – and I know
you'll never make me better
any more. I feed
the warmed sweet almond oil

with a dropper
into my dead ear
and feel the good oil
opening the wax.

In four days time
I'll hold
the white enamel kidney bowl
against my neck

while the huge syringe
shoots water
down the auditory canal.
At first it thrums

like a far-off city
and then the whole live ocean
rushes in.
Afterwards,

in the mild November dusk,
I sat in the park
and watched two bats
suturing

the darkening air,
their zigzag flight
latticing the stark
and emptying trees

with a fragile network,
an impossible filigree
that fails
as it describes

their hunger close to night.
Their sight is sound –
those high-pitched cries
light up the chestnut trees

with call and echo,
making feeling
from reflection –
and I can hear them!

There, right at the edge
of sound,
like a quill on glass,
an exquisite engraving

that I thought
I'd lost forever.
I raise my fingers
and I rub them

near my mended ear
to hear that precious music,
the pitch of flesh
on flesh.

Spilt Milk

Two soluble aspirins spore in this glass, their mycelia
fruiting the water, which I twist into milkiness.
The whole world seems to slide into the drain by my window.

It has rained and rained since you left, the streets black
and muscled with water. Out of pain and exhaustion you came
into my mouth, covering my tongue with your good and bitter milk.

Now I find you have cashed that cheque. I imagine you
slipping the paper under steel and glass. I sit here in a circle
of lamplight, studying women of nine hundred years past.

My hand moves into darkness as I write, *The adulterous woman
lost her nose and ears; the man was fined.* I drain the glass.
I still want to return to that hotel room by the station

to hear all night the goods trains coming and leaving.

In Passing

I cannot now remember
　　how I came to be waiting
　　　　on a bench in a car park

at the back of a station
　　in the suburbs of Philadelphia
　　　　twenty-six years ago –

strange, American weeds
　　lifting the pocked asphalt,
　　　　a mongrel asleep in a rusting trolley,

the tired light a hive of dust motes
　　thronging the limp damp air
　　　　of a late August heatwave.

I had never been alone,
　　so far from home, before,
　　　　observer of these passing,

ordinary lives – the wonder
　　of finding myself, here,
　　　　out of place, unobserved.

I stepped on the platform
　　just as a goods train passed through.
　　　　The length of it winded me –

boxcar after boxcar after boxcar
   furiously intimate, close enough to touch:
      the whiplash of turbulence,

the aftershock of silence.

Travelling Northward

through the worst March snowstorm
anyone on this train has ever heard of –
Water Street in Bridgeport, Connecticut
is stopped, a quilt of ice –
only the restless and the homeless
risk the streets tonight.

This train, like any train
I've ever taken anywhere,
moves from metropolis to detritus,
its trajectory –
from dressed-stone, steel-clad, po-mo vaults,
heated, peopled, electronic,

to those laid-off warehouses,
their tall machines eviscerated
left to breed a skin of verdigris
against the open, negligent air –
is voodoo economics stripped:
the counting-houses, gilts and deals

are come to this –
a rusting chain-link fence
around an empty lot,
two huge cogs lying out of gear,
fabulously swollen with the snow.
The stilled train

creaks a little to itself, then leaves
New Haven, all but two carriages
plunged into darkness
(there now are nine of us),
the steady veil of snow
covering our tracks, clinging to

the gargoyle icicles that rope-
off the carriages, glaze the metal stairway
with a skid of glass.
I don't know where I am.
I can only match the cold-occluded signposts
with the Amtrak schedule in my lap,

to plot this journey to new weather.
Two hours ago we left Penn Station,
tunnelling through Manhattan,
then emerged – where? –
was that the Bronx below me?
the rigid grid of houses

grilled into the distance
by a futuristic blueprint years ago.
Nothing balks this weather:
the heedless, desperate cars
abandoned, slewed across
the streets at random,

their gases and their deadly engines
made benign by sheaves of whiteness.
This is not a pastoral.
The snug, urbane, well-heated
Amtrak train I'm travelling in
mechanically performs its engineering feats:

balancing these thousand tons of metal,
plastic, humans, glass
across a cantilevered iron bridge
forged a century ago,
behind which fumes a power station
sixty metres high, one huge wall a window

golden, molten, transfigured by its power.
Electricity. Its nineteenth-century
narrative of hope for some
is giving out. The cold comes down.
The journey from James Watt's boiled kettle
to this insulated Amtrak train

seems evolutionary, tracked and planned.
I read the signs
but don't know where I am.
Outside there is a bonfire in a parking lot,
a group of cold men pressed together
round its light.

The Maryland State Penitentiary

For three nights I slept in a room
with a view of the Maryland State Penitentiary.

That huge cathedral of punishment
held its bulk against the winter storm,

its thickened walls immune to snow, to cold,
the falling snow small flurries

in the steady yellow floodlights,
their untroubled gaze

fixing on the big walls and the bars,
one gothic window tall enough for prayer.

My window also has its bars –
wrought-iron, sculpted, almost elegant –

to keep the outside out.
The frozen metal burns my palms.

*

A year ago I worked Inside.
The night I left,

I stood in the abandoned Education Block
and breathed in that sour, cooped-up air.

I memorised the worn-down walls,
the braggadocio and the insults carved on desks,

before I locked those dank and straitened rooms.
In the narrow corridor

I pressed my face against the filthy, meshed-in windows
to stare at a view that would not change:

the half-demolished prisoner-of-war-camp buildings
jutting concrete, wires, mesh and rusted bars

out into the weather.
Then I wandered through the darkened prison,

unlocked, then locked, the heavy gates six times,
handed in my keys, and left.

          *

Tonight in Baltimore
I slip the latch and let the cold come in

to see if I can see a window that a prisoner could see through –
to watch the storm come down

or, if gazing at the city spread beneath him,
could glimpse this small and distant building

these red-brick walls, my tiny square of light,
almost hidden

by the endless, falling, freezing flakes of snow –
but there is none.

Proof

Your abandoned bottle of Russkaya vodka lies in my icebox,
Cold as a gun; it will chill but not freeze,
The slow distillation latent beneath the iced glass.

Wolves Are Massing on the Steppes of Kazakhstan

Close to home, their prints
darken the snow.

Come full moon,
the whole night is anguished –

cattle
stagger in their sheds

knocking the walls,
churning fodder and litter;

wide-eyed in lamplight
they buck and bruise.

Under Stalin
culls worked like clockwork –

wolves skinned from their pelts
were hung out to dry,

as cotton stretched to new horizons,
as Kazakhs ate the dust.

Now fences are mended
bolts shot home

and the shotgun propped
by the bed

is oiled and loaded.
But sleep, sleep is fitful

as the wolf packs mass
on the steppes of Kazakhstan.

The Garden of the Virgin

'In the Gospel of the Egyptians ... the Saviour himself
said, *I am come to destroy the works of the female.*'
— CLEMENT OF ALEXANDRIA, *Stromateis*, Book III

I

Fearing the approach of his second death,
Lazarus – he who had known the chill
of the tomb, who had felt the soft worms
weld to his flesh – Lazarus, the Bishop of Cyprus,
requested the Virgin's blessing. He sent
a boat for her, and Mary sailed from the coast
of Palestine – the clear sky big with itself,
the sea blue as the sky – till a storm drove
her off course, and she came upon her garden.

II

From the far northern coast
of Greece, from the low
treeless shore of Halkidiki,
three arms of land slide into
the Aegean Sea.

From the edge of the third
Mount Athos pierces the sky,
its darkening, gashed
escarpments finished by
a crest of white.

Below, the isthmus falls away,
its rough spine a wood as dense
as any fairy-tale, as thick
with wolves. The forest of Athos
is pungent

with the gums and oils of pine,
of juniper and thuja, is massed
with ilex and arbutus,
with the loose mauve flowers
of the Judas tree.

III

At Clementos, Mary
alighted
into recognition.
The Pagans fled.

In their makeshift
shrines, the idols
of their female gods
debased themselves

before her, imploding
into dust. The Virgin
walked through Athos
in the cool of evening,

inhaling its aromas,
gathering the blooms
of oleander and hibiscus.
She declared this garden

her domain, declared
(recalling Eve)
no other female
should come to foul

this paradise.
Then she left for Cyprus,
for the final death
of Lazarus.

IV

The monks who came to cultivate
the Virgin's garden
obeyed her law.

St Theodosius the Studite wrote:
Keep no female animal
for use in house or field:

the holy fathers
never used such –
nor does nature need them.

Ewelambs and their ewes
were slaughtered. Cows
butchered. Heifers slain.

The sow, the gilt
and the nanny goat:
all dead and banned.

Bitches murdered one
by one. Each hen
felt the press of thumbs

about her throat, the neck
snapped taut – and then
the slump. Each egg

was gathered up, each eggshell
crumpled in a viscid mess of yolk,
thrown oozing down the cliffs,

where, boiling in the waves,
it made a salty broth
the gulls sucked up.

Only the cats stayed on:
the cats to catch the rats
that dropped their young

despite the monks,
despite the Virgin's stern
injunction. At night

it was the cats
who ran the place:
softening the hands and throats

of anchorites and cenobites,
their lithe fur
soothing the flesh made stiff

through deprivation.
And at night the wolves
roamed yowling

through the Virgin's garden:
the sole beast
with cunning enough

to breach the fine neck
of the isthmus.
Miles up, alone

in his stone cottage,
reached only by chains
hung over cliffs,

a hermit wakes up, sodden
from a lycanthropic nightmare,
with his hair

on end. He had sensed
the slow breath
of the wolf, had stared

deep into her lemon eyes,
as still as oil
or candlelight, then

felt himself run off with her –
feral, hirsute, opening out his lungs
to greet the moon.

Petersburg

for Ruth

A week with no stars.
A week with the full moon occluded by light.

At midnight, the Winter Palace is on fire –
one thousand molten windows

scarlet with the agonies of sunset
igniting in the west.

I run across the Palace Bridge
into the origin of red,

intent on the bloodied winding cloth
of a day that's refusing to die.

City giddy with light,
balancing water with granite,

urgent with traffic pounding
this bridge that, soon, will throw up its arms

to let the night ships glide to the north,
heavy with exchange.

City of ghosts, familiars, lyrics –
and words, mouthed into stone.

Transparent Petropolis, absolute beauty
is a shard of glass snagging the heart –

the subjects of imperial architecture
are cancelled by the fury of scale.

These infinite vistas master the Neva
in a hard embrace – its bedrock

the countless hands of slaves,
impossibly gilded, furnishing the swamp.

This is the illusion: perspective is everything.
Wherever I may stand,

the vanishing point is my eye,
the beholden.

Lunatic

We have sexed
A sterile rock rambling through a frigid night,
Relinquished wombs and cycles

To her span,
Made our receptacle for moods eccentric
To the shift of clocks.

Essentially
I am a tide, dependent on your flex and lapse –
A pendulum of blood.

And though obtuse
And punctual I wander through these rational streets –
Still some nights you heave

Silvered
Through this mottled glass, when I confess my gender
To your lucid gaze

And crave asylum in such lunacy.

Medium to Fine-Grained Vesicular Crystalline Rock of Igneous Origin & Concrete

for Niall McLaughlin

When I was twelve men landed on the moon. Awake till dawn,
I watched the TV with the sound turned down
show pictures of Michelin Men,
light-headed,

fumbling over rocks: their masks of glassy black reflecting back the
    moon, the gleaming
moonscape yawning
into darkness – and at its edge
the sickle earth

veined with clouds and oceans, the two man-made walls
you can see from outer space. Afterwards
I watched the moon slide out of
my window:

she was still the same as yesterday, with half her face opened to the
    night. A girl at
school said, *You don't believe
they've been there? They filmed it all
in Hollywood.*

But then I saw the moon rock: just after Christmas I queued for hours
at the Geology Museum to gaze at
a piece of the moon
so small

I could put it in my pocket. It lay under a huge curved dome
of glass, poised in silver tongs, each pore freckled
with crystals winking out at me.
All week

we've watched the break-up of Berlin: the wall split open
by bulldozers and cranes, the patience
of a thousand chisels tapping
through the night.

And now you're back from Potsdamer Platz with your gift
of concrete: I hold the Berlin Wall
and feel its roughness
warm my hands.

November, 1989

A Fistful of Foraminifera

Sand, at first glance –
granular,

a rich grist
of grains and slim seeds,

opening
into a swarm of small homes

painted rose or ochre, saffron, chalk,
some blown steady as glass –

hyaline, diamond,
the pellucid private cradle of a tear.

    *

The balanced simplicity of a singlecelled cell,
busy with its business

in absolute silence.
Pseudopodia

float
clear through their apertures,

banners coursing the waters,
furbelows, scarves, ragged skirts;

brief tactful netting,
shy gestures of touch.

Their filigree mansions
are chambered with secrets –

auricular passageways
give onto galleries,

soft arcades,
furrowed with arbours, open

onto balconies, that lean
over doors, propped ajar.

*

Benthic,
their galaxies carpet the depths of the oceans,

a slow chalky ooze
bedded down softly in darkness.

They conjure their houses
from flotsam and jetsam,

tucking grains closely
between alveoli,

secreting a hardy, calcareous mortar;
the shell walls buffed till they shine

or pebbledashed sugary white –
the architectonics of happenstance and grace.

*

Pennies from heaven,
the yellowing bedrock

hewn into slabs
is stuffed full of treasures.

Slipped from their homes
come hundreds of coins,

big stumbling sovereigns,
pocketfuls of pocketmoney,

fit for flipping, fit for hoarding
in chests.

Nummulites gizehensis,
the wealth of the pharaohs

is hauled up heavenwards,
a limestone staircase to the stars.

*

Tumbleweeds, spacecraft, seedpearls, squid,
fairylights, pincushions, biodomes, sheaths,

colanders, starfish, thistledown, dhal,
powderpuffs, ammonites, cornichons, teeth,

puffballs, longbones, condoms, bulbs,
thermometers, pomegranates, catapults, hail.

*

Open your fists
and the mortal remains of one million creatures

will spill
through your fingers –

Eocene
dust in the wind.

Tidemarks

The seaside out of season: it's pissing down.
At equinoctial low spring tide the beach is nude,
the rocks stripped back,
barnacles left sucking at the air.

These ordinary limestone extrusions
are salt-dark from their dealings with the tides,
are rimed with spiralwrack and thongweed,
pitted into rockpools;

and the one I'm mirrored in's
a small home
to a solitary sea anemone
shrugging its undulant, rose-hued fronds for food.

Rounding the headland twenty years late
nothing has changed,
only the cedar of Lebanon has stretched to shield
the red-brick crenellated miners' rest home

from the restless waves.
The posh hotel has held its corner;
next the stolid row of big
bay-fronted bed-and-breakfasts

curves down to the front.
Months ago, the heath was burnt;
and now the tarmacadamed path
bisects the heather, gorse and broom

the startled undershrubs caught petrified,
their gestured arms in flight,
wrought and blackened by the heat.
Further on fresh shoots break through,

the yellow lips of gorse blooms
easing through the burl of spines,
the fine pelt coated with the salty rain.
The scorched earth smells of artichoke.

At seventeen I hadn't seen an artichoke.
Nowadays I've learnt the ritual
of stripping back the tight-packed petalled head
to unsleeve the longed-for heart,

and to abjure the feathered needles of the choke,
its iris tempting and implacable.
At seventeen I wondered why
the sand below me

slipped beyond the small vocabulary
I tried to dress it in
of platinum and mushroom, oyster, eau-de-Nil –
till dusk fell and the tide drew in

to wash the shades away.
In the cupboard on the stairs at home
a Huntley and Palmers biscuit tin
is labelled 'minerals' in my cursive, adolescent hand.

I opened it last week
and found I knew each rock,
its journey and geography, each given name –
feldspar, jasper, tourmaline or quartz –

carefully printed
then stuck down with strips of yellowed sellotape
the decades have transformed
into another mineral –

mica, isinglass,
the lifted texture of an insect's wing.
And now I trace myself across the sands
away from crowds and relatives

searching for the certainties of crystallography.
I find the place I prised a vein
of milky quartz
out from its bed of carboniferous limestone,

its cold hexagonals
opalescent, almost perfect,
each crystal spawned from an ideal form
its flawed, unkiltered rhomboids

made opaque by slip and circumstance,
so knowable and mineral and hard
against my palm.
In books of crystallography I found

its history, its structure and its family
reduced to letters, numbers, symbols
that evaded me.
I dreamt of schist and basalt,

malachite, obsidian and marble, jet;
undressed each landscape to its geomorphic curves,
saw glaciers and slow moraines
ease the valleys opened, fertile, wet,

drumlins scattering in their wake.
I knew the sucking clay of London
dropped beneath my feet.
One day I would be mineral,

my cold bones leached of flesh and hair
crumbling into soil.
I came here out of season once before,
my Irish grandpa with one green eye and one blue

was dead, and I sat out the funeral on this bench
seeking comfort in these cliffs and headlands,
the loved, familiar bay,
the flux of its geology

incremental, fixed, beyond my mortal eyes –
not knowing I'd return two decades on,
sit down here and take in this landscape,
collect myself, then turn back in the rain.

Morphology

At a quarter past three
the bottom shelf gave up,
casting its yellowed magazines
and tampons to the floor –
and that marble egg
which split in two,
revealed itself
as thickened marble,
pink and veined with
dirty cream, all through.
I long for a geode –
some simple rock
that would admit a heart
of amethyst or malachite –
or the pebble
that you found in Brighton,
an ammonite:
the intricacies and volumes
of its life
expressed as a skeleton,
worn in stone.

The Fracture Clinic

The weather broke the day my parents met me:
after an early spring the air turned hard; drizzle;

the gutters blocked with blossoms of the palest pink.
They climbed the big stairs to the Priest's house

in St Charles Square, and found me silent in a cot.
Then they named me, took me from a Home to *home*.

At twenty-one I found the mother I had never known,
much smaller than I'd thought, her hands like mine.

Too much dancing, she told me. Saturday nights
she'd sneak out the back, her black pumps in a paper bag,

and take the bus to town. One night in June,
with all of Dublin lit up, spread beneath her, she fell

pregnant, then lost me in West London to the Church.
Last Saturday I danced too much and fell.

They have taken me to St Charles Hospital
where I drowned in anaesthesia: beneath a star-shaped atrium

I watched the milky light turn crystalline, then I went
under. Now I'm lying in Recovery,

my wrist encircled by my date of birth, my postcode
and my name, all written upside down.

My Father's Piano

Carved from the seasoned hearts of rosewood –
    the fine grain veined black
        through the sheen of maroon –
    my father's piano
        was the centre of home;

the sounding-board of thought and feeling
    ignited by
        the heartbeat, heartbeat, heartbeat
    threading through the scales
        of pitch in time.

Look at it unpacked –
    a junction box of forged connections,
        the waves of felts
    in red and green and deep sky blue,
        the interleaved shanks,

the hammers and dampers, stacked and packed in
    as close as a skeleton,
        stitched through with steel –
    the plumblines of tension –
        the strings spun around

their curved constellation of chromium pins
    scattered on a sky
        gilded Krugerrand gold.
    Always I was staggered
        by the deep bass darkness

catching at my heart, resounding around
    my lungs and bones,
        by the tinsel glissando
    housed in high ivories
        at the edge of sound –

the hammers' attack on the strings forging joy,
    then tempering tenderness.
        This is the work of love –
    the testing of harmonies
        through the risk

of dissonance, trying again as the hands fall apart,
    taking on silence
        when the afternoon fades –
    practice and grace,
        as light ebbs away before tea.

Small Rains

After all these years
you still fracture my sleep:
I am lost in a cold bed,
my mouth wrought into bitterness.

I imagine you awake at this hour:
your cigarette starring the darkness,
lulled by the small rains
that settle on Dublin –

as I lean from a window
in a night with no moon
and watch the street lights
ebb into dawn.

From Dublin to Ramallah

for Ghassan Zaqtan

Because they would not let you ford the river Jordan
and travel here to Dublin, I stop this postcard in its tracks –
before it reaches your sealed-up letterbox, before yet another
  checkpoint,
before the next interrogation even begins.

And instead of a postcard, I post you a poem of water.
Subterranean subterfuge,
an indolent element that slides across borders,
as boundaries are eroded by the fluency of tongues.

I send you a watery bulletin from the underwater backroom
of Bewley's Oriental Café,
my hands tinted by stainedglass light as I write,
near windows thickened with rain.

I ship you the smoked astringency of Formosa Lapsang Souchong
and a bun with a tunnel of sweet almond paste
set out on a chipped pink marble-topped table,
from the berth of a high-backed red-plush settle.

I greet you from the ranks of the solitary souls of Dublin,
fetched up over dinner with the paper for company.
Closer to home and to exile,
the waters will rise from their source.

I give you the Liffey in spate.
Drenched, relentless, the soaked November clouds
settle a torrent of raindrops
to fatten the flood.

Puddles pool into lakes, drains burst their sides,
and each granite pavement's slick rivulet has the purpose of
    gravity.
Wet, we are soaking in order to float.
Dogs in the rain: the cream double-decker buses steam up and
    stink

of wet coats and wet shopping,
a steep river of buses plying the Liffey;
the big circumnavigations swing in from the suburbs, turn,
cluster in the centre, back off once more.

Closer to home and to exile:
I seek for this greeting the modesty of rainwater,
the wet from ordinary clouds
that darkens the soil, swells reservoirs, curls back

the leaves of open books on a damp day into rows of tsunami,
and, once in a while, calls for a song.
I ask for a liquid dissolution:
let borders dissolve, let words dissolve,

let English absorb the fluency of Arabic, with ease,
let us speak in wet tongues.
Look, the Liffey is full of itself. So I post it
to Ramallah, to meet up with the Jordan,

as the Irish Sea swells into the Mediterranean,
letting the Liffey
dive down beneath bedrock
swelling the limestone aquifer from Hebron to Jenin,

plumping each cool porous cell with good Irish rain.
If you answer the phone, the sea at Killiney
will sound throughout Palestine.
If you put your head out the window (avoiding the snipers, please)

a cloud will rain rain from the Liffey
and drench all Ramallah, drowning the curfew.
Sweet water will spring from your taps for *chai bi nana*
and not be cut off.

Ghassan, please blow up that yellow inflatable dinghy stored
in your roof,
dust off your compass,
bring all our friends,
and swim through the borders from Ramallah to Dublin.

Swimming to Spinalonga

for Crispin

At dusk I watched you swim to Spinalonga.
Sitting in the bar at Plaka

I felt the glass of ouzo
cool against my palms;

the hard ice loosened,
bled the liquor white,

until its clarity had turned opaque,
until I held a glass of milky quartz.

I looked up and you were yards out,
your sleek head

a needle
suturing the navy waters.

Along the shore
big granite pebbles

exhaled the whole day's heat
like fresh loaves just tipped from the tin.

The tamarisk tree kept its own counsel,
its dense laced fronds

harbouring a coolness
all day long. For half an hour I lose you.

The sickle moon's no use,
her paltry beam

illuminating nothing but her bony self,
and Spinalonga island is a distant darkness.

Forty years ago I would have looked upon
an awkward constellation of small lights,

pinpointing deportation,
the bright stigmata

of the colony of lepers
banished there,

these calming waters
a no-man's land they died to cross.

The place has been cleaned out now:
the disinfectant room,

the cisterns and the laundry
no longer function.

Three days ago
I took refuge from the fevered sun

inside the old taverna,
its walls undone,

the plaster flayed right back
to rotted slats,

the roof defeated.
But away from glare and weather

was a frieze of cobalt blue,
the intricate flowers and fruits

were steadfast
where the stones had met and held together.

I took the rusted window clasp and pushed
the shutters back: in the courtyard

a cuckoo Yucca
bulked against the garden walls.

I found you at the graveyard,
the tombstones shattered

exposing whitened skulls,
the longbones

of four hundred lepers
whose journey ended here.

The night comes on:
small stars of jasmine

let go their piercing scent.
I watch the dark sea gather

and relax,
then find its rhythm is you swimming back to me.

Climbing from the water to dry land,
you paint the grey stones inky

shaking off your skinful
of the salty sea.

Cotton Boll

From here, the cotton fields stretch further than an ocean,
undulant green, pocked with foam.

Little bush, burning in the catastrophic heat,
how far did you come

to set root in this thick black earth, humidity rising,
staggering belief?

Sheets, winding-sheets, underthings, handkerchiefs –
a polity of garments

spun from that one fine thread, yanked
straight out of your heart.

Dyed, dark-stained with sweat, how invisible is the yarn
that ties the weaver to the woven

when all we grasp is stuff –
the loosening fabric of desire, or of utility,

that we labour to possess, unlace, discard,
then burn.

The Florist's at Midnight

Stems bleed into water
   loosening their sugars
      into the dark,

clouding dank water
   stood in zinc buckets
      at the back of the shop.

All night the chill air
   is humid with breath.
      Pools of it mist

from the dark mouths
   of blooms,
      from the agape

of the last arum lily –
   as a snow-white wax shawl
      curls round its throat

cloaking the slim yellow tongue,
   with its promise of pollen,
      solitary, alert.

Packed buckets
   of tulips, of lilies, of dahlias
      spill down from tiered shelving

nailed to the wall.
　　Lifted at dawn,
　　　　torn up from their roots

then cloistered in cellophane,
　　they are cargoed across continents
　　　　to fade far from home.

How still they are
　　now everyone has gone,
　　　　rain printing the tarmac

the streetlights
　　in pieces
　　　　on the floor.

African Violet

Tender and cautious,
shipped north across continents,

the African violet
blooms into mildness –

seeking the equinox,
patient, till day

balances the night.
Hirsute secret hoods

ease back
the gauzy, veiled flesh

to a star of opening mauve,
pierced at the heart

with sheer gold –
pollen sacs hidden and swollen.

Neglected in winter
the furred leaves fur with dust,

with trails of lint,
with a lost web going nowhere.

Little succulent overlapped and stacked plates
the leaves rosette from their roots;

crimson of the vulnerable underleaves
intimate as a mouth.

Plunged under water
the flat leaves are aglitter –

small cells full of air
picketing the hairs,

till jostled
they seethe aloft,

freckling the meniscus
with burst.

Snapped, the rich veins ooze
their glossy ichor;

laid onto loam
the tiny adventitious roots

furl through the soil,
shaking a new plant free within weeks.

The Physic Garden

1.

Hard to have faith in these twisted dry sticks
crusted with rime;
hard to believe that roots
still web the blank soil of the Order Beds.
Species and genera,
a crop of old labels bedded in iron
their stalled limbs aimed at an empty sky.

2.

A cold spring, a late spring.
Reticence, patience.

Fresh leaves risk the weather.
The first primrose burns.

All of the daffodils
arrive all at once.

3.

Nothing is written
on the leaves of the bluebell,
blank strips of green
fallen back on the grass.

The flowers cluster and rise:
mute mauve fingerstalls –
a knee-high haze
under sycamore and oak.

4.

Disease infuses
the garden's roses
as a fungus pools
around the stilled blooms.

5.

Look, even in July,
the leaves of the
Liriodendron
are learning to yellow:

lemon and gold
leavening the green.

6.

Someone is burning
the last leaves of autumn.

The veil of sharp musk
unfurls through the shrubbery,

the sweet aroma of loss
stinging tears from my eyes.

7.

This, then, is dusk in the garden:
light fled

to a honeycomb of yellow
where the gardeners have gone

to clean soil from their tools.

8.

Even in the still centre of the high-walled garden
paradise is contingent.

On a bench in the dark
the hurt roar of traffic batters the night;

one jet a minute landing at Heathrow.

9.

Journeys taken so long ago
the seeds sow themselves

turn weedy
escape

Trotsky's Garden

I wanted to stay in Trotsky's garden,
to sit out the hot day
under the banyan tree,

to find names for the cacti and climbers and shrubs –
the Siberian irises over, cut back for the year,
the scarlet banana

a lit fountain of gold in the sun,
the neat disciplined lawn with its long snaking hose
coiled in the afternoon heat.

I wanted to stay here till sunset,
to witness the sun
as it skirted the walls to pace out the garden,

to feel night closing in,
the huge pull of the city heaving and teeming,
the life of the city as remote as the stars.

*

When Lev Davidovich
fled to Mexico
with Stalin's dogs snapping at his heels,

he fetched up here –
in this *little fortress* in Coyoacán,
the *zone of coyotes* as it's known to the Aztecs.

The suite of small rooms, half-walled with glass,
is left as he left them.
His old straw sombrero, his walking stick, tossed

on the iron-framed bed;
a fleet of black typewriters on bare wooden desks;
a wall map of Mexico;

yellowing pamphlets in Russian,
in Spanish, in English, in French;
mismatched china and earthenware crockery

and a caddy of Queen Mary tea
in the doll's house-sized kitchen.
His passionate library locked up for good.

*

Nothing else can survive under such harsh conditions:
the absolute zero of night in the desert,
the searing cauldron of noon.

Leaves abandoned for spines and needles.
Fertile soil scorned.
Cocoons of white hair.

Moisture lured from the air
and laid down in sacs,
plumped tissues swollen and secret and viscous.

Columns and barrels and disjointed joints,
taller than palaces
or less than a pebble.

And the absolute triumph of glorious blossoms
cast off at dusk
when no one's to notice –

cerise, tangerine, scarlet, chrome yellow –
the shocking waxed petals flare out of nowhere,
hyperreal, burning and utterly still.

                    *

Because now there's nothing to be done
but wait for bad news to turn worse,
for the worst to come true –

L D's absorbed by his cacti collection,
furtively culled in raids staged at midnight,
while his guards

cock their weapons and scan the horizon.
Look, here he comes
over the brow of the hill for the very last time,

the moon breaking clear of the clouds –
triumphant, filthy, and happy as Larry,
wrestling a huge blue agave back to the car;

big fists of soil thump the ground as he walks,
his face lit up,
a pickaxe slung under one arm.

Chinampas

The Floating Gardens of Xochimilco
are all that remains
of the wild surmise
of Hernán Cortés
when he first saw Mexico –

Tenochtitlán
the great city of canals
of islands woven from grasses and mud
balanced on willow roots
reaching right down to the pith of the lake

A backwater now
a suburb pitched on the edge of town
scene of outings on the *chinampas*
for the tourists and locals
thronging the gondolas

A little boat punts by
laden with pot plants for sale –
an unsteady *Washingtonia*
fans open its one pale palm
in surrender

My Grafting Knife

A whole week's wages
balanced on my palm

The cherrywood clasp
burnished and finished with brass

Lockjaw
I unjoint the heart

and the steel heart
arcs

from silver to blue
hurting the air

The fine blade cleaves
to the whetstone

first a dry rasp grates
the granular carborundum

then the whispered finesse
of the oilstone filmed with oil

Six strops on the leather strap
I could carve

scarves of gossamer tissue
One poised gesture

and the ichor oozes
The knife stop – my right thumb

crisscrossed with hair-scars
tarnished with sap

Jasmine in Yemen

In the Friday prayers' gridlock
a man with a *djambia*
and a cheek full of *qat*
casts a garland of jasmine
through the shattered car window.
Luck and friendship.
A heady necklace of deaths
looped round my shoulders,
the sharp pungent blooms
fighting the tang of exhaust
and spent oil,
the funk of blown meat
from a plague of pink plastic bags.
Soon the flowers will bruise and fall.
A circle of string left hanging on a doorknob.
Lost petals where I strayed
from the balcony to the bedroom.

Gardenia

One lopsided, scorched-brown bloom
then refusal on the kitchen windowsill.

Symmetrical and silent, the glossy pools
of leaves bisected into light and shade,

the nubbed buds stubborn,
green as leaves, crouching in the foliage.

Faking patience, the north light is
luminous, whitening as the spring comes on.

Once I turn my back, the flowers untwist
in hours, fattening with odour,

with the heady heat of flawless whiteness.
The carved, curved geometry of the blooms

more lucid than hallucination.
As simple, as thoughtless as a bruise.

Rosemary

The small sprig crumbled in my pocket
tucked inside my old blue jacket
hung up in the closet the whole winter long.

Plucked from the tall bush by the garden gate
the glaucous spikes,
the sheer blue flowers just starring into bloom.

Even now, the faint, insistent scent –
a slim tincture of openness,
stringent and clear.

No-one saw me leave the garden.
No-one knows.
And now, the tendril powders in my hand.

Hibiscus

I have no idea what is coming
   as I take the hand of a perfect stranger
      as I'm taken through the streets of Marrakech.

The exhilaration of trust.
   The exhilaration of risk,
      of balance –

of balancing on the back of his Vespa like a teenage lover,
   my hands gathering his jacket at the waist,
      learning how to give round corners,

forgetting the crush of traffic from nine directions,
   forgetting the chaos at crossroads,
      my cheek now on his back,

the disinterested city
   open before us,
      passing me by.

We loop away from the Djemaa el Fna,
   we loop away from snake-charmers, pet monkeys, jugglers,
      beggars, fortune-tellers, water-sellers,

tagines and harira and brochettes,
   from strings of white lightbulbs,
      from the scent of burnt charcoal

burning the night up all night long,
   we loop away from the slipper souk and the silver souk,
      from the Koutoubia Mosque,

from the Kasbah Mosque and the El Mansour Mosque,
    from the palaces, all the palaces,
        from the medina which now I will never walk through,

from the gardens closed for the night.
    We loop away from that one huge bud of hibiscus –
        madder red, almost cerise –

that is, at this minute, coming full into bloom,
    opening its impossibly crimson throat wide open,
        now, in the dark, before midnight, exactly,

that one hibiscus bloom,
    the one I could have gazed at, gazed into,
        eye to eye

drinking in its throat,
    its scarlet throat,
        its stigma and stamens just risen,

pushing from the petals,
    out of the petals into the night,
        vulnerable and slender and scarlet,

the anthers swollen, dusted yellow with pollen.
    That one hibiscus blooming in a garden
        I will now neither visit nor know

– while I weave through traffic with a stranger,
    our words swept up by the wind
        and thrown off into the night.

I am balancing.
   I am laughing.
      I am lost in the suburbs of Marrakech.

The city is a tent.
   The city is a rose tent.
      The low rose buildings pleated together,

the castellated walls smoothed out of mud,
   the wide boulevards spinning off into the desert,
      streetlights painting the rose walls

with slashes of amber and bronze,
   white streetlights,
      high up, threading the boulevards,

spinning them into the night, into the desert.
   We are camping in the desert.
      In a desert scented with orange-blossoms,

with the first flush, the young flush of the earliest jasmine,
   with date palms to guide us,
      with date palms pushing up higher

than the rose-coloured buildings,
   higher than the haze of charcoal and spiced food,
      their huge crowns crowning Marrakech,

their stately crowns swaying in the breeze
   that shifts down from the mountains.
      And we sway through the city, bending and circling,

passing all these people I will never greet –
   the men in white shirts talking on corners,
      the women in djellabas going home with the shopping,

the women in djellabas riding on mopeds,
   headscarves like banners
      streaming behind them,

four boys in an alley playing football
   with a football with a puncture,
      and the old man in the kiosk

where he picks up the key,
   while I straddle the moped
      shifting warm metal from right thigh to left thigh,

absorbing the glances,
   the half-curious glances,
      shot at a white woman in this end of town.

Not much further.
   The rose buildings are concrete, closer together.
      We lift the bike up under the stairs

then climb them in darkness,
   hand in hand, feeling the walls,
      right up to the roof

to a room loaned for the night;
   a room with a mattress and a candle and a radio
      (a radio which, in Arabic then French,

will murmur of disasters just out of my grasp).
    When he leaves me to piss
        I go to the window

to map out this journey, to find Marrakech,
    and I pull back the shutters,
        the stiff slatted shutters –

and there, between the slats and the glass,
    balanced on less than one inch of sill,
        is a bird's nest.

A bird's nest woven of a filigree of fine straw
    and cardboard
        and small curled grey feathers,

with two eggs,
    two cream and brown-speckled eggs,
        nestled together in the cup of the nest,

warm and oval and whole.
    I watch these eggs until I know them.
        I watch the lights of Marrakech

high above the buildings rise up to the stars.
    I watch Marrakech
        through this dusty windowpane,

through a window with a crescent of glass
    snapped off at the root.
        Then I close my eyes

and ease back the shutters.
    I return to a room I will never return to
       and I kneel on the mattress.

All night the radio loses the station
    to a whisper of static,
       the soft cry of crossed songs.

Communion

I

We both might wonder what you're doing here
till you take refuge from your hunger in my fridge
and then come out with something

that we share the name for; *choriço picante*.
I watch you pierce
the raw meat with a fork

and hold it in the naked ring of gas
until the skin is charred and blistered black
until the stove enamel's measled red.

Slit it down the side
and open out its bleeding heart –
ruddy, vivid, rough.

II

We cannot speak each other's tongue
and so you open up your shirt
to give me signs, to show your wounds.

I know this much:
that, as a child, you fled to Lisbon from Luanda
with a bayonet wound a foot long

(never sutured)
that now grows on your arm
as though a snake's embossed there;

that your skin was punched with shot
which, ten years later, form the dark stigmata
branded on your legs and arms.

III

Take this pungent flesh into your mouth
and staunch your hunger.
Eat.

Or a Line of Lemon Sherbet

The edge of Tunisia is like the sea-side
or an abandoned set from *Beau Geste*.
It is one hundred and ten degrees.
You eat pilchards on Ryvita
and long for a sorbet
or the beginnings
of a pier.

By the time you reach the Tademait Plateau
all the hairs on your body are bleached
to the last shade of straw. Here even
your shit is a landmark. Heat bends
the horizon of ochre and orange
under a muscular sky.

Near Tamanrasset you find a spring of fresh
fizzy water. Plunging your arms into
this cold spawn you feel its gases
tick along your wrists.

The Hoggar Mountains are white on your map,
their lavas stunned into gothic bosses
and sills – cathedrals without relics
or candlesticks. You cup your palm
round an elbow of basalt and
search for your echo.

Then you meet a hermit carrying a gas-cylinder.
For thirty years he has lived where no-one
has lived, among lava and stars. His
plastic sandals are beginning
to give at the heel.

Pause in the *feche-feche* and you drown.
On your right is a blue *deux-chevaux*
up to its knees. Then the emptied
suitcase and one sling-back shoe
losing its grip.

Each night you sleep out under a big sky
and watch the North Star slip out of
reach. You envy the confident moon
intent upon leaving.

At three o'clock the night loosens its stars like
spilt salt. How you long for one to lighten
your tongue like a line of lemon sherbet
or a eucharist you could take and tuck
behind your teeth.

Eighty miles from Agadez you unscrew the last can
of spring water. You hear the dim hiss of
one thousand miles north. Small bubbles
freckle your mouth.

May Day, 1986

(for Tadeusz Sławek)

Yesterday, the weather in Warsaw
was the same as London's: *Sunny, 18°*
(sixty-four Fahrenheit). I am sitting
in a walled garden drinking gin,
the fading sky as blue as this tonic water
loosening its bubbles against the flat ice.

What is in the air? The first midges;
a television three doors down, its hum
like this lone bat avoiding the walnut tree.
A dog barks. In other houses lights come on –
the street an Advent Calendar opening
its doors. This house is in darkness,

its seven windows admitting the night.
I'm trying to read *Mansfield Park*, to learn
how Fanny finds love and a mansion
through keeping silent. All week
the weather report has plotted the wind
leaving Chernobyl with its freight

of fall-out: cancer settling on Poland –
the radio-activity an inaudible fizz
in the cells, rupturing thorax or liver,
the intimacy of the bowel. They say it won't
reach here. I stare at the sky till all
I can see are the dead cells of my eyes,

jumping and falling. It's too dark to read –
only the flare of a late *Kerria japonica*,
trained to the wall. I think of your letter
in my drawer with the handkerchiefs,
one page torn by an earlier reader. Socrates
distrusted writing, its distance from

the grain of the voice. I come indoors
to write you all the things I couldn't say
a year ago. Later, on the news, they will show
gallons of contaminated Polish milk
swilled into sewage, a boy crying
at the sting of iodine he must swallow

against the uncertain air.

Ramallah

Freezing out of season
with Eid after Easter

– a provisional city
a concatenation

of loose roundabouts
building sites

and razor wire –
scars of forced demolitions

spite
occupation and new wealth

Little Bantustan
rimmed twice with checkpoints

claustrophobia
of the stone's-throw distance

disconnected phone lines
no phone lines

and roads
stopping short

Hard-core and gravel
a job-lot of kerbstones

wires spewing from snowcem
as frozen rain fumes up

the broken street
Rattling windows in the teashop

jammed shut with old rags
steamed-up with the steam

from *chai bi nana*
from the honey tobacco

of ancient *nargilas*
from gossip and politics and love

The dank rotting theatre
perished through

with thirty years of enforced
darkness

Plush slides
off the chairs

dust rots through the curtains
and every human breath

exhales its weather upwards
in a cloud

I never found the centre
just a ring

of handsome policemen
dressed in blue

March, 1997

Landscape, with Dead Sea

for Izzat

Flat out on brine
    at the bottom of the world –
        not one wisp of cirrus

can mar the lapis lazuli dome
    cupped over this dry bowl of hills,
        pastel hills folded in stillness.

Buoyant on bitterness –
    the tonnage of fluids transfigures
        into haze above my very eyes,

to a mist heavy with elements,
    molecules of sweet water
        shipped up slowly to infinite blue.

These deep, barren waters
    are riddled with toxins and salts.
        At the shoreline I harvest

the dark, sybaritic mud –
    worked into my flesh, its granular
        astringency erodes my dead skin.

Down south, Potash City –
    acres of evaporation pans
        and chimneyed factories,

ringfenced depots stacked up with acids,
    with phosphates in boxes
        and sulphurous drums.

At sunset, the western, volatile sky
    ebbs through carmine into mauve.
        The lights come on in Jericho:

I imagine what I cannot see –
    barbed wire threaded with jasmine,
        sharp enough to smell.

This riven land: here
    the great tectonic plates glide asunder
        as fast as my fingernails grow,

riding the molten core of magma –
    the invisible, radiant heart of the earth,
        burdened by geography, charged with life.

Zaatar

Astringent, aromatic, antiseptic –
the souls of the dead
come to rest in the blooms
of this bitter herb

to haunt the bleached landscape
of limestone
of broken stones
of olive trees stricken and wasted

Incendiary – a volatile oil
can be crushed from its leaves
small pockets of scent
toughened, hirsute

Uprooted, exploded
ground under foot
its pungency rises
staining the air –

pollen like gunpowder
dust in the hand
cast over Palestine
from the mouths of stones

Glaucium flavum

Yolk broken on the shingle,
a cadmium flag –
five silken petals
flourished by a sharp November breeze.

Beached on detritus,
sheltered by the litter of Seablite and Stonecrop,
the Yellow Horned-poppy
finds shelter on rubble,

harvesting moisture
from dewdrops latched between stones.
Split, the plant exudes
a toxic yellow gum,

that's stowed in hirsute leaves
against the saline plague of the sea.
Its seed pod, a curved, black bean,
is a torn claw, vacant

as winter knuckles down.
Beyond Thorpeness
rear the bulbous, concrete tanks of Sizewell,
hatching reactions, collisions,

staining the tides with their alien warmth.
Yet still the sea repeats
its old declensions,
rubbing armfuls of flints into grit,

then sand,
making dust to be swept off by winds
when the land is barren
and the coastline gone.

Damascene

Centuries of barefoot pilgrims have walked
this white marble to the stuff of glass –

billowing, doubled in *hijab*, I look down
into the heavens' absolute descent.

Swarming aloft from the rink of the Umayyad Mosque
a dark crowd of pigeons rips

open the fabric of dusk –
figures scaling the last slow heat of September,

a heat heavy with the end of a summer's summer –
its dust now settling onto cupolas and pantiles,

onto the balconied, octagonal minaret
where Jesus, one day, will alight to bring Judgement.

In the greenish, underwater gloom of the Prayer Hall
the head of John the Baptist waits behind bars.

*

How strange I am to myself here –
out of bounds, unknown.

Lost in the night streets of Damascus
I am a figment of shadows

cast by yellowing lamps
down pleated corridors of overlapping homes;

their whitewashed flanks are still warm from the sun –
breathing, intricate, woven from wattle and thatch.

    *

In a room walled with carpets,
a room warm with the smell of shorn wool

and the metallic tincture of dyes –
he laid me on a *kilim*, and I bled.

Dust

I hold the condom to the light
the still-warm cells seething and dividing

There's a bleached aroma with a rim of zinc
– like a sixpence hidden in your mouth

In ten days time
the thickened lining of my womb

will loosen turn to blood
between my legs

A decade more of this
and then I'm finished

Cells are leaving my body
the fine dust in the sheets

the grey dust on the high shelves
the lampshade

the mauve dust ravelling into nests
under the stairs by my old winter shoes

pollen on the windowpane
as the maculate sky gives into dusk

Europe

Merely an idea bruising
the far horizon, as a cold mist tightens into rain –

but at dusk we still wait
by the Bay of Tangier, on the old city walls, gazing
   northwards

till the night comes on,
and a necklace of lights gathers the throat of the sea.

The young men burn –
lonely, intent on resolving that elusive littoral

into a continent of promises
kept, clean water, work. If they stare hard enough, perhaps

it will come to them.
Each night, they climb these crumbling ramparts

and face north
like true believers, while the lighthouse of Tarifa blinks

and beckons,
unrolling its brilliant pavement across the pitiless Straits.

Mahbouba Zaidi's Hands

slip into mine. She leans me against
a smooth, cool pillar
and takes my waist in her arm.

Her hair is in my eyes. Her dry brow against
my lips. We have walked at midnight
along slim paths of plaited stone,

leaving the streetlights for darkness.
The other tourists are asleep. The Sicilians are dreaming.
My palm traces the muscles of walls

softened by a millennium of palms and shoulders.
Her hip presses into my hip. Her spine is under
my fingers. She leads me through Erice

to the Castello di Venere. I want to tell her
that Daedalus came here, bringing a honeycomb
of gold for Aphrodite, honouring her shrine,

but there is nothing between us but broken
Italian, schoolgirl French. I understand
how she will come here at dusk

and lean out into the still, aromatic air, searching
for Africa, for a glimpse of the rim of her home:
a dim, glaucous haze sixty miles distant,

a continent away. Tonight there is nothing but blackness
and stars. Later she will lead me to the hotel
and slip in through the back. *Rosa*

the owner calls out, asking where she has been.
They have changed her name. *Hush,* she whispers,
It's far too complex.

Passages

Decree: clear skies
over the heart
of London: cirrus,

nothing less
flaming
the far edge of blueness,

nothing less
marking
the absolute boundaries

of air, of resolution.
A cast of slowing jumbos,
emptied of fuel, begins

the descent:
trawling
the long southern flight path

down into Heathrow.
When the huge wheels
hatch

from that cold,
aluminium belly,
will a petrified figure

plummet down
(this time)
into a carpark,

breath frozen midair,
the wrapt human form
congealed

on the landing gear
tossed three miles clear
from touchdown,

from migration?
The big silvered craft
run the gamut of light,

taking in evening
buoyant, journeyed:
pushed to the edge

of the city: now exposed,
with its parcel of lights,
its human freight

inching homewards
through dusk, mid-September,
as fear

slips its cold roots
through the known.
The dull muddied Thames

is full of the equinox,
dragged by the moon
the dun waters

flush to the Barrier:
a ruined city checked,
a whole rumoured ocean

balanced in abeyance.
Tides dissolve memory:
history

loosens its cargoes
into the tides'
heedless swirling,

forgetting,
heading out to the open.
But the silt sifts on,

turning and sorting:
as the docklands drop
out of sight,

cargoless,
trafficless, winches abandoned,
ceilings undone

to the skies.
And the skies are rivers
freighting

the burdens
of rivers: transhumance
precious and raw

now landing on tarmac.
The jets tick
as they cool,

boxes contracting
on earth,
as rivets ease back:

the hulk
emptied of passengers
now filling

with migrants:
labouring in the site
of exile and arrival.

The swallows
left weeks ago,
with no notice:

one afternoon
the skies
were abandoned:

lack
takes them southwards.
And in the formal garden,

the last hybrid roses
flare rose-pink and
salmon and mauve,

but the sap's on the turn.
And the earth is balanced,
day equalling night:

and is equally
unbalanced
as rumours are pieced

into news.
After this: winter.
The youngest vixen repeats

her sharp scent,
doubles back, excited
back again,

crouching,
back now to the rough path:
slips

under the light paling fence
and is
gone:

The Jardin des Plantes

Do not go to the Jardin des Plantes.
The false acacia has shed all its leaves.
The cedar is threadbare. The avenue
of lime-trees is an avenue of stumps,
lopped limbs prickling with hapless twigs.

Do not go to the Jardin des Plantes.
Instead, stay here by the river.
Stay here and keep vigil for that man
on the Right Bank who is losing his mind.
There, at the lip of the Seine, beneath

the oblivious, continuous traffic,
watch him pace his stone stage, half-naked
at freezing point, haranguing his invisible familiars,
beating the insensible concrete with his fists.
January. The river cold as a blade.

The suffocated sky like cotton-wool wadding.
Stay here and watch. Kneeling, then flailing
at the wall. Beseeching the water. No one
knows you are here, observing a stranger
in agony across the river. Do not go

to the Jardin des Plantes. The cactus house
is closed. The order beds are bald.
The rheumy-eyed pansies leak back into the soil.
Little cloches abound, cosseting the feeble
under sweating, grime-streaked panes of glass.

Meanwhile, there is gravel. Meanwhile,
everything you love is staked up, cut back or
dead. And now the wind is a weapon.
The weather is a weapon.
A basketful of knives spat in your broken face.

Alone in a city of pursed lips, abandoned by a river
that knows nothing of the tides, a river
unlatched from the moon, a river too far from the sea.
So face the implacable river, Left Bank/Right Bank.
Face that man a hundred yards off, that stranger

cursing this bitter dusk.
Do not go to the Jardin des Plantes.
Stay here on these steps till darkness is absolute,
till nothing can be seen of that figure at the river's edge,
of a woman eclipsed.

Total Eclipse

I have travelled this far: to a stubbled field in a foreign land;
the heavens above, a cold bowl full of clouds.

We are pilgrims seeking portents through the prisms of science.
Earthbound: the sucking clay soil doubles my boots.

Eclipsed: abandoned. The unpredicted has finished my heart.
And the weather itself will brook no prediction.

Seconds away, a black tornado is scouring the earth.
No revelation: just absolute darkness at half-past noon.

The dead cells of my eyes double and swarm, seeding the clouds
as the inexorable calendar ticks through my heart.

I submit my evidence: of what I could not see coming.
I recall my memory: of what is finished.

Solstice

The solstice sunset of the final summer of this thousand years
finds us silent, side by side, divided by the dateline.

The earth has turned its back: the swollen sun
is swallowed by the dome of the Observatory.

The Thames at Greenwich is a beaten platinum ribbon
coiling through the city, unspooling to the teeming sea.

The rose sky's turning mauve, then violet, then midnight blue.
But look at London kindling the night: each lit light an act of faith.

The grid of it: crossroads, junction boxes, wired-up and fused;
and the trains without drivers are crossing the city all night.

Because I am fallen, I must fly down this hill.
Because I have lost you, I must take up this thread.

Almost the Equinox

and the Thames so emptied of current
it shows bare flanks of sand. Beige sand. A beach.
The sudden vertigo of hardness when we're cupped
over the walls of the Embankment

examining the strange cream stones below,
driftwood, bottle-tops, crockery, one sodden boot.
And the slow mud opens its mouth.
Jets long departed, their contrails fire

across the fierce blue skies, unfurling
into breath. The very last weather of a summer
spent impatient for change,
waiting for a sign, an alignment.

Beneath our feet, a hemisphere away,
the full moon tugs fluids into tides, and stops
another night in its tracks,
hours before it climbs over London –

the constant pull of elsewhere
mooring us outside ourselves. The colchicums
come naked into the early autumn air.
Bruised into mauve and purple,

their frail blooms admit the memory of harm
in their risky flight to beauty. Packed bulbs
underground harbour their secrets.
Now that we have witnessed

the flare of that ginkgo spilling up
besides St Paul's – its roots woven
deep beneath a graveyard of graves,
its slim knotted branches, sleeved

with airy, fantail leaves –
it will return to us, suddenly,
years from now. Anomalous Jurassic relic,
its origins are as ancient as these slabs

of blackening Whin-bed Portland Stone,
set here by Wren to stamp out Fire and Plague.
As a child, I climbed all the stairs
to the Whispering Gallery, laid my cheek

against the painted plaster of the dome,
and let those perfected acoustics bear my changed voice
back to myself. The huge nave
reminds you of the Great Mosque in Kabul –

sunlight falling on pillars of stone, the hushed intentness
of prayer. Shattered, war-torn, it's still standing,
somehow, next to the river by the Bridge of Bricks,
just as Wren's great dome once soared above the Blitz,

intact. Tonight, we will look up to see
Mars, that old harbinger of war, come so close to us
it rivets the southern sky with its furious,
amber flare. Sixty-thousand years ago it lit

these heavens and looked down
on ice. Next convergence, nothing will be left of us
leaning on this bridge of wires and tempered steel,
wondering at the river and the city and the stars,

here, on the last hot night before this planet tilts us
into darkness, our cold season underground.
The tide has turned, the Thames comes inching back,
drowning everything it will reveal again.

for Yama

The *Sand Fulmar*

Squat, the flat shade of sand-
flats, docked west of Woolwich,

the *Sand Fulmar* waits
to be emptied:

of silt, of erosion, of friable shale
bled down to riverbeds:

a mobile geography
shipped from estuary to factory.

After twelve hours
all the grains are spooned

clear of the hull,
crowning a huge mounting dune

crawling up skywards.
Tonight,

the full hull of the dredger
is heavy as a river:

the Thames elbows its flanks
and streams on.

A school of orange buoys
winks, as the high Thames churns

seawards:
burst flowers of lights

bloom and split
while the tide plies the currents:

but the dredger won't budge,
absorbed with its load,

silt
hoarded up to its gills.

Two big cartwheels of paddle flats
with rough shovels attached

plunged deep under water,
hauling marl

from slowed sand-banks,
brackish juices

spilling down
the chins of the buckets,

set free to flow onwards,
lured by the undertow.

Now, at the depot's edge,
soft migrant grains

will bed down in darkness,
a promiscuous mingling

of mica and silica,
of small bones and smashed shells,

of beachglass and rock quartz,
with sandworms,

with seaweeds
torn up from their roots.

Once the huge tube is screwed
into place

the granular cargo
is parcelled along

a once-cream-painted
busted and rusting conveyorbelt

twenty yards high,
to dust the new landscape

mounting behind the locked chainlink fence.
In the factory of aggregates

tall vats of spent oil
stand by shy growths of ragwort

or rosebay willowherb,
the sharp tang

of coaltar staining the air.
These are the journeys

of the slow hearts of rivers
turned stubborn with silt:

dredged clear, transported,
they will curdle in bitumen.

Sealed drums of asphalt,
stirred into pitch and mixed up with sand,

wait to be fired,
to be laid down as roads.

The Foot Tunnel

for Andrew

The dream always dreamt just before dawn:
walking the cool white tunnel to its end,
pace echoing pace,

the chill white tiles streaming with breath,
with rumours of the Thames
(its brown tons of water and cargoes,

its river creatures, silt) dragging above us,
pointing the walls with a century of damp.
We pass through a ghost-mist, drawn on

by a row of dim lamps pinned to the ceiling
pulling us downwards through walled-up clay
deep underneath the cold throat of the river.

Spilt out of the wood-panelled, rickety lift
we are shocked by air, by seagulls soaring and diving,
by the world swivelled round, clouds, the sudden

smell of the sea. We have walked under
water, to be drenched to the bone
by a joyful June downpour, punched from the skies.

The Grass Church at Dilston Grove

Papered with clay
then seeded with fescue and rye,

the church walls fur
with a soft green pelt,

filaments trying the air
before climbing the light.

The church is damp;
it smells of a tool-shed:

mineral,
soil coating tines and boots,

vegetable, with the sap
of lifted plants.

At sunset
small squares of yellowing sunlight

plot the grass as it fades
through cross-hatched windows,

loose panes stove in,
the lead curled back.

Memories of redemption
wane in the rafters,

communion forgotten
in the emptied nave,

a mission beached
without a flock,

the lost souls lost
to the docks.

Pebble-dashed agglomerate:
these are the rough-cast walls

of the first concrete church in London.
And now the grass comes home

as a box of green metaphors
opens

while I watch.
How old I have become.

Everything the grass has asked of me,
I have done:

I have taken the grass for my path,
for my playground, and for my bed;

I have named grass seeds,
I have borne volumes of turf;

I know the stuff of clay,
the weight of sods,

the bloom of *Agrostis*
on mended soil.

Everything the grass has asked of me
on this earth, I have done

except give my self
up

except lie
under its sky of moving roots.

Watershed

Overnight, *Bellis perennis*
would heave its fist of leaves
up into the light
rupturing the bowling green.

In the flat heat of the afternoon
I knelt in my small shadow
puncturing the hard earth
with a dining fork,

attempting to unseat
the urchin daisy from its home,
its nude roots woven in the soil,
the pink-flushed blooms

slim embryos, packed within
the tight-whorled leaves;
then I tucked the new seeds in
to mend the wounded soil.

This was the summer
when you could fill your palm
with grass seeds
and I'd know their names:

Festuca rubra commutata
(Chewing's fescue)
Festuca rubra rubra
(strong creeping red)

and *Agrostis tenuis*,
its gentle growth as fine
as baby's hair.
It never rained.

The longest drought since
records began. All July
the tight sky banged above us
all day long.

My reddened shoulders
turned to skin; detached;
a loose, translucent parchment
that streamed off,

frayed, and blossomed
in my twisted sheets
as dust. At work
I learned to use

the Ransomes Auto-Certes;
each week my boss would tinker
with it upside down,
tickling the carburettor,

feeding slips of cartridge paper
into the hive of sharpened blades
until it sliced them
into perfect squares.

Three times
he let me carve the lawn
into its warp and weft,
the shaven grass striped green,

then lighter green,
then green again.
No girl has ever done that,
he told me, when I stopped for tea.

Some of the Bowling Club
are blaming you for this
he gestured at the sickening lawn.
My sex could blight

their turf. Turn milk
foetid in an hour.
It never rained. By August
we were mowing down the soil.

We gave up watering after eight:
the moisture either dropped
straight through the ground,
or simply turned to steam;

so I rose at four,
watched Venus slip
behind a block of flats,
and left for work.

The dawn released the fragrance
of the lime-flower trees
which cloaked the long,
cool avenue I walked along;

the half-light lifted,
the distant trees, the lawns,
first grey, then glaucous;
the bowling green,

the porter's lodge now
breaking into form.
It never rained. I learned
the fungal sicknesses

of turf by heart:
Fairy Rings, Fusarium patch
(its pink mycelia
like cotton wool)

and red thread
(corticum disease);
in the half-light
of the musty shed

gleamed poisonous tins
of malachite green
to wipe them out.
The *Salix tortuosa*

lost its leaves and died;
its twisted branches
made an absent *haiku*
against the naked wall.

Only the Giant Hogweed
thrived, spawning
by the putrid riverbank,
its bloated umbels

carried twelve-foot high
by hollow stems
hairy and maculate,
harbouring a vicious juice,

cousin to the Hemlock
and to Cowbane, to the deadly
Hemlock Water Dropwort.
It never rained.

Each night at home
I found the small rooms
stiff with heat,
the hard air

tight against the glass.
I was nineteen. Waiting
for the sky to open.
I washed my shirt

and watched it dry
from navy into sapphire
in an afternoon.
Across the estate

two dogs were fighting.
I heard the ice-cream van,
the children I no longer
recognised clamouring

outside the flats.
No-one called all weekend.
I slept through Sunday.
That night I climbed

the ten flights to the roof
and out onto the flat
expanse of asphalt.
It warmed my back.

I had never seen
so many stars,
so old, so far away,
shining down

their messages of light
from centuries ago.
I didn't know
the constellations,

I lacked the skill
to make the stars reveal
their names and myths –
until one

slid then hurtled
down the sky. Next day
the floods came down.

Heavenly Body

I could stake out the summer at my kitchen window:
   scanning the street,

searching for the scarlet flare of your Mercedes at my kerb.
   Since St Swithin's Day

it's pissed down. On August 12th the world's astronomers
   observed the Perseids,

expectant that Swift-Tuttle's comet dust would storm
   to starlight.

But in Notting Hill the clouds occlude the heavens;
   the passing cars

in darkness turn anaemic, their lights a sallow blur
   along the seething road.

The Mist Bench

Even at night, at random
a click
– and mist fumes

from the watchtowers
clouding the cuttings
with fog

Bare leaves are downy
turn blurred
and glaucous

as the fine fur plumps
and sleeves itself
with water

Ten beats and it's
finished
The electric leaf

buried in the leaves
is parched
and replenished

all night

The Growing Room

Lux eterna:
the Dutch lamps
beam all night

Walls of loam
shelved in green trays

Dicotyledons
breaking the surface

dense as a rain forest
glimpsed from a plane

Begonia seeds
are costlier than gold:

I tweezer open
the cellophane envelope

unhouse the blond dust
inhale

then waft
the precious cirrus

softly
down to earth

Year-Round Chrysanthemums

In mid-July
they think it is winter

All it takes
is an hour's incandescence

at midnight
and their day

germinates: twenty-four hours
makes two

Year-round chrysanthemums
the long nights

make you rich
and fecund

Your bunched, curled faces
magenta and saffron

phototropic with desire
inexorably riding the light

No. 3 Greenhouse, 7.30 a.m.

Genuflect
crossing the threshold

The unopened air
heady with the odours
of cloves and roses

The carnations are speechless
Candles
ascending the nave

(So easy to befuddle –
remember ink in the jamjar
the pinked frills taking blue)

They must lose their heads
before they turn spray

I stub out the buds
A twist and they're single

Auxins surge from the one heady flower
the bouquet's darling

Cloistered in glass
I am taken by ritual
postulant to the blooms

The Tree Bank at Ten

The long stretch till lunch
after the miles
back from tea-break,

mist cured away
by the bald, implacable sun
– and nothing but tasks,

tasks, in this factory of trees
which are not trees
(*Aesculus, Tilia,*

Ulmus, Acacia)
but tagged products
notched down

the poisoned clay road,
template of rank
and infinity.

Raffia balled in one pocket,
the hard knife hasped
shut in my fist,

I must ship up this pickaxe,
arc it
down in cold clay

till my spine is a fine blade
of fire
and both palms

sting in the morning air,
as I stretch up
to catch

the reinforced windows
of John Conolly's crenellated
Hanwell Asylum,

as in turn I'm surveyed
by a whey-faced crocodile
of long-term patients

gingerly tracing
Brunel's redundant
Grand Union Canal

before lock up. Before lunch.

Umbellularia californica

My lodestar,
the headache tree,
has plotted this garden –

the shy silver birch
placed in its shadow,
the ornamental waterfall

just so,
making fake waves
on a beach of big pebbles,

one lone mallard
motoring
the Japanese pond.

Decades ago
its slip
crossed the Atlantic,

tough thongs of roots
keeling down
through dark loam.

Now, once more, I am
flat out
on a slab of oolitic limestone,

absorbing the dusk
leaking blue
through its tall net

of branches,
the three-pronged trunk
a plumbline of evening,

those swarming
black leaves
fingerpainting the sky.

What unguents beat
through its
heartwood?

What alchemy
forges
those naphthalene leaves? –

slim, dangerous bay leaves:
torn
they let go

an odour
as heady as camphor,
tightening the third eye,

a poultice for the fury
of the mind
drawn into one point.

Once done,
the dusty brown scales
are shoaled

into hiding,
or taken by the wind
tick tick along the path.

Even the flowers
are secret: pale
yellow umbels

show at the cusp
of winter,
way out of reach.

Cynosure reeling me in
since my teens,
my life

graven
in that rough bark
furrowed like the seabed

pleated by waves,
the history and memory
of all these sunsets

transformed into cambium,
laid down
in rings.

I come here
not for a cure
(analgesic, demulcent)

but for a witness,
for the process
of a map.

Colchicum (The Autumn Crocus)

Shivering in September
   they come out of nowhere –

ghost-blooms –
   their slim flames flaring

in the shrubbery
   at dusk.

Petals the exact shade of pink
   bred under fingernails,

or the mauve of a bruise
   pressed on pale flesh,

or the dead-white of milk teeth
   tucked close to the bone.

Flayed by the rain,
   in October

they are litter –
   ruined things

splayed amongst the leaf-mould,
   the heavy petals

all keeled over,
   their etiolated stems

flat out at random.
   The rot sets in –

dark spots foxing
   the torn inflorescence,

the whole border gone.
   I could talk to you

of resurrection,
    of fat corms fattening

overwinter in the dark,
   of the long straps of leaves

which unwind, unremarked,
   in the spring, on their own –

but not now.
   This is the time for grief,

to look carefully at loss,
   then turn away.

Cow Parsley, Bluebells

for Kathleen Jamie

Waist-height,
clouds of white lace
in the abandoned graveyard,

the delicate,
filigree umbels
matching

the thumbprints of lichen
embroidering the graves.
A deep current of blue

surges below –
bluebells,
moments of sky

fallen,
brief weather
fixed on wet stems,

conjuring a climate
gone from this chill April dusk,
as rain comes, and light fades.

Vigil

Late June, the night air stitched with the scent of lime-blossoms.
When you left, these trees were bare.

The last swallows at nightfall: their perfect parabolas of hunger and
    grace.
Each year, only days after they have gone, do I notice they have
    gone.

Fox on the path: wild creature, at home on the cusp of the city,
how long will your gaze lock onto my gaze?

I measure out the cloth to sew a new cover for our bed:
the warp and weft of fabric, its journeys, the places we will meet.

My body alive with your voice.
The phone warm in my hand.

Yards away, the alluvium of the Blue Nile plies the White Nile's silt.
Pull your bed into the courtyard and sleep under a blanket of stars.

Leaving Omdurman, the moon journeys northwards. Hours later,
I stand in her platinum light. Searching her face for your face.

Notes

'**The Pomegranates of Kandahar**' – This poem was prompted by an item on BBC World Service Radio, broadcast in January 2002, about the legendary orchards of Afghanistan. The most delicious pomegranates in the world were once grown in profusion in Kandahar province.

'**The Invisible Mender (My First Mother)**' – The haberdasher's on Chepstow Place opened in 1914 and, when I knew the shop, seemed little changed since then, the shop fittings and some of the stock dating back to the First World War. The tailor J. T. Morgan took over the shop in 1980 and ran it until rent increases forced him to close in 2001.

'**Travelling Northward**' – 'voodoo economics' (a term coined by George H. W. Bush) refers to the disastrous economic policies of Ronald Reagan (and Margaret Thatcher) that hard-pruned state spending and delivered tax cuts for the rich.

'**Wolves Are Massing on the Steppes of Kazakhstan**' – Headline of a report on BBC World Service Radio filed by their Central Asia correspondent on 15 January 2000.

'**The Garden of the Virgin**' – 'An Orthodox spiritual centre since 1054, Mount Athos has enjoyed an autonomous statute since Byzantine times. The "Holy Mountain", which is forbidden to women and children, is also a recognized artistic site.' (UNESCO *World Heritage List*)

'**Medium to Fine-Grained Vesicular Crystalline Rock of Igneous Origin & Concrete**' – Title taken from a postcard of the moon rock first exhibited at the Geology Museum in 1970: 'Collected Apollo 11 site, southwest Mare Tranquillitatis, July 21st 1969.'

'**A Fistful of Foraminifera**' – Commissioned by Robert Crawford for the 'Contemporary Science Meets Contemporary Poetry' project supported by StAnza. The poem emerged from a collaboration with Professor Norm McLeod, Keeper of Palaeontology at the Natural History Museum; I am deeply grateful for the encouragement, insight and information he gave me.

'My Father's Piano' – Commissioned for broadcast by BBC Radio 3 in the *Poetry Proms* series 2000; the programme was produced by Fiona McLean. Many thanks to Stefan Jacubowski of Blüthner Pianos, Berkeley Square, London W1, who kindly dismantled an upright for me.

'Swimming to Spinalonga' – Spinalonga, a small island north of Elounda in Crete, was a leper colony from 1903 to 1957.

'Trotsky's Garden' – After twelve years on the run from Stalin, Leon Trotsky finally found refuge in Mexico in 1937. In 1939 he moved into the 'little fortress' at Viena 45 in Coyoacán, a quiet suburb of Mexico City, where he was fatally attacked on 20 August 1940. Whilst in Mexico, he became a keen gardener and developed a passion for collecting cacti. See Isaac Deutscher, *The Prophet Outcast: Trotsky 1929–1940* (Oxford: Oxford University Press, 1963), p.448. Strictly speaking, an agave is a succulent not a cactus.

'*Chinampas*' – The canals and 'floating gardens' – *chinampas* – of Xochimilco are what Mexico City (Tenochtitlán) looked like at the time of the Spanish invasion.

'My Grafting Knife' was manufactured by TINA of Germany. In 1974 I was earning around £20 per week as an apprentice gardener with the London Borough of Ealing, less than the price of my knife. In 2015, a TINA grafting knife could be bought for about £60.

'Jasmine in Yemen' – A *djambia* is a heavily-ornamented – and extremely sharp – curved dagger worn by Yemeni men. The leaves of the *qat* shrub (*Catha edulis*) contain cathinone, an amphetamine-like stimulant, that's released with prolonged chewing.

'*Zaatar*' is the Arabic word for thyme (*Thymus vulgaris*) and is the plant most strongly associated with Palestine, where it grows in profusion.

'Passages' – 14 June 2001: 'A stowaway on an aircraft coming in to land at Heathrow fell to his death in a Homebase carpark yesterday . . . It is thought that the stowaway fell as the pilot of an unidentified jet lowered the aircraft's landing gear. Police said the man was of Mediterranean or Middle Eastern appearance, in his late twenties or early thirties. He was wearing black jeans and a shirt and carried no identification.' *Aviation Security International.*

'The *Sand Fulmar*' – A hopper dredger launched in 1998, the *Sand Fulmar* still journeys between the sandbanks of the Tyne and the aggregate plants of north Greenwich, unaware that it inspired a poem.

'The Grass Church at Dilston Grove' – In October 2003, the artists Heather Ackroyd and Dan Harvey created a remarkable installation by sowing grass seeds all over the walls of the deconsecrated church in Dilston Grove, Rotherhithe. Formerly the docklands' centre for the mission work of Clare College, Cambridge, this pioneering concrete structure was designed in 1911 by Sir John Simpson and Maxwell Ayrton. Since 1969 the building has acted as a gallery and studio space for a number of artists.

'Watershed' – *Bellis perennis*: the common daisy, a weed from a bowling green's point of view. The bowling green I cared for during the summer of 1976 was in Pitshanger Park in Ealing; it was allowed to become derelict and now no longer exists.

'The Tree Bank at Ten' – The London Borough of Ealing's Tree Bank was situated on a strip of wasteland just outside Southall, west London, between the Great Western Railway and the Grand Union Canal. John Conolly (1794–1866), the most important early-Victorian psychiatrist, was responsible for introducing a benign and humane regime to the large public Hanwell Asylum during his period as superintendent there between 1839 and 1844. The old building still stands and, during the time the poem is set (1974–77, when I was an apprentice gardener with Ealing Parks Department) it was known as St Bernard's Psychiatric Hospital.

'*Umbellularia californica*' – The Californian Laurel, or Headache Tree, gets its common name from the pungent aroma released by crushing its leaves; opinion is divided as to whether the smell actually causes headaches or relieves them. Herbalists use the leaves as an analgesic and a demulcent. The plant was introduced to Britain by David Douglas in 1826. This particular tree, now brutally pruned back, can be found in the Japanese Garden in Holland Park.